# Word of the Week

# Contributors

Karen S. Gillman

Mark Gillman

Laura Hart

Jessica Santiago

Lauren F. Sheridan


#onpoint

#weop

# Dedication

This book is dedicated to all the authors and publishers who have participated in the On Point Book Fair.  **You inspire us.** We hope this book of words will do the same for you.  You keep writing and we will keep reading!

A logophile or a philolgos is a lover of words. A logomaniac is a person who is obsessively interested in words.  We consider ourselves to be all in the same.

If you use one of words from this collection in your writings, drop us a note and a page number.  We would love to quote it on our social sites!

# On Point Book Fair

The  On Point Book Fair began in 2015 when the planning of one author's personal book signing blossomed into a celebration of writing for 50 local authors.  Karen S. Gillman published her first book titled, It's Never Too Late, A Journey With Weight Loss Surgery and planned an intimate book signing to be held on Rocky Point, Tampa FL.  When a fellow friend/author heard of the planned event, they asked if they too could host a signing for their book.  Karen's philosophy was, 'the more the merrier'.  Within a few short weeks, the event filled to the venues capacity and the evening consisted of 50 local authors.  The next year the event moved to the WestShore Plaza in Tampa, FL and doubled in size.  Now, authors, publishers, bloggers, graphic designers, editors and vendors line the hallways of the Plaza for a one-day annual event that locals look forward to.

A $1,000 Business Builder Grant is awarded to one author each year and is designed to provide a ' business boost' to take their writing journey to the next level.  The grant is provided by Fulfill Your Destiny and is a highlight of the event!

www.facebook.com/onpointbookfair
www.onpointexecutivecenter.com/onpointbookfair

# Apropos

Definition: Just right, appropriate in a specific situation.

Examples: That blog post on terms of service was apropos, considering the changes many of the sites have made in the last month.

She had nothing to say apropos of the latest developments.

# Judicious

Definition: showing good judgment;
wise.

Examples: He gave a fair and
judicious summary of all the matters
properly to be considered, and I
find no misdirection of the law.

Having numerous perspectives from
informed members of the community
will allow for an educated dialogue
and, ultimately, a judicious
decision.

# Abhor

Detest something, to disapprove of or reject something very strongly.

Examples: Many students abhor learning history because there are too many dates and facts to memorize.

I abhor when people do not read provided instructions.

# Insular

Definition: separated and narrow-minded; tight-knit, closed off.

Examples: Moreover, few outside influences had ever been incorporated into this music, making this a very insular culture.

One interesting case is the assimilation of foreign cultures that took place in insular Southeast Asia.

# Catawampus

Definition: askew; awry,
positioned diagonally;
cater-cornered.

Examples: The canoe lies
catawampus at the entrance to
the cellar.

The papers were shoved catawampus
into his desk.

# Forelsket

Definition: the euphoria you feel
when you first fall in love.

Examples: My son is in High School
and has experienced forelsket with
the new girl in his class!

At the risk of sounding prideful,
my husband had an extreme case of
forelsket when we first met!

# Brusque

Definition: rudely abrupt or blunt in speech or manner.

Examples: It's notoriously easy to hit the wrong tone and come off sharp, imperious or brusque in e-mail when you don't intend to.

The staff was treating her in a very brusque and insensitive manner, and I felt the need to show her some warmth and caring.

# Cacoepy

Definition: incorrect pronunciation
or an instance of this;
mispronunciation.

Examples: Errant pronunciation
guides may lead to cacoepy.

The word 'tomatoe' is often cacoepy.

# Lurid

Definition: ghastly, sensational.

Examples: Dr. Ink grew up reading, and loving, the New York tabloids, so he has a taste for the lurid and sensational.

By that point, however, the audience is accustomed to lurid details that toy with the established presentations of the play.

# Myriad

Definition: consisting of a
very great number.

Examples: It centers on a central
ingredient such as eggplant, okra,
spinach, quince, celery, or a myriad
of other possibilities.

Fast-flowing rivers create
spectacular waterfalls, gorges and
a myriad of caves.

# Capricious

Definition: given to sudden
and unaccountable changes of
mood or behavior.

Examples: Since she is known
for capricious behavior, Katie's
friends were nervous to tell her
the bad news.

A child's mood is capricious.

# Nominal

Definition: trifling, insignificant.

Examples: The local jeweler will
do it either free or for a nominal
charge while you wait.

A nominal fee is charged for a range
of odd jobs around the home, such as
mending dripping taps or fitting
lightbulbs or smoke alarms.

The On Point Book Fair charges a
nominal participation fee making
the event affordable for all
authors.

# Immersion

Definition: the action of
immersing someone or something
in a liquid. Deep mental
involvement. Instruction based
on extensive exposure to
surroundings or conditions
that are native or pertinent
to the object of study.

Examples: We were surprised by
his complete immersion in the
culture of the island.

He learned French through
immersion.

www.facebook.com/onpointbookfair

# Bots

Definition: a bot, otherwise
known as a chatbot, is a type
of software designed to automate
tasks over the internet that are
ordinarily handled by humans.
They often operate in conjunction
with instant-messaging platforms,
and got a huge boost when Facebook
opened up Facebook Messenger to
third party bot development.

Examples: For now, the bots respond
to questions on specific topics.

The shopping bots show price
comparisons for items matching
your description.

# Taciturn

Definition: not inclined to talk.

Examples: He was a rather taciturn individual who discouraged chatter in the theatre.

Friends described him as reserved, almost taciturn, but insatiably curious about science and technical processes.

# Plethora

Definition: a large or
excessive amount of something.

Examples: Grand Cayman offers
a plethora of bustling restaurants,
ritzy resorts and comfortable
condos. There has been a plethora
of plays in recent years whose
claim to modernity is based on
indicated rather than felt
emotion.

# Truculent

Definition: ready to fight, cruel.

Examples: Perhaps all this success and recognition has softened what was once a rather truculent disposition.

She was very argumentative and truculent and when I tried to calm her down, I noticed something strange.

# Cacophony

Definition: an unpleasant mixture of sounds; harsh noise; discord.

Examples: Sometimes it seems as though the dogs in our neighborhood bark together to create a cacophony that wakes me up.

A cacophony of bleats, chomping and scuffling of hooves drowned out her words.

# Garish

Definition: showy; over decorated.

Examples: They climbed the garish purple-carpeted stairs.

Her hair has been dyed a garish shade of red.

# Cajole

Definition: to deceive by flattery;
coax.

Examples: By telling her husband
how handsome he looked while
cooking,

Helen was able to cajole him into
making her favorite meal. Aid
workers do their best to cajole
rich countries into helping.

# Insipid

Definition: without flavor; tasteless.

Examples: The soup lacks the right seasoning and tastes insipid.

Jackie could think of nothing more insipid than watching cartoons with her younger sister.

# Foible

Definition: A weakness or
eccentricity in someone's character.

Examples: She loved him in spite
of his foibles.

The man could tolerate his
companion's foible because it
was covered by her many admirable
qualities.

I have accepted the fact that I
will remain this weight, my foible
for food is uncontrollable.

# Umbrage

Definition: resentment, offense, annoyance.

Examples: There was a silly argument and Coleman took umbrage at Mr Clarke's tone of voice.

He does not take umbrage at the incongruous presence of the housekeeper in a presidential suite that is still occupied.

# Misanthrope

Definition: Someone who dislikes people in general.

Examples: Freud was not only a misogynist but also a misanthrope.

The old man was a misanthrope who surrounded his entire yard with barbed wire to keep his neighbors at bay.

# Salient

Definition: significant, conspicuous.

Examples: Population and employment are more concentrated in Dublin and therefore childcare is a salient issue for more people.

The bloggers scour far and wide for news reports and bring the most salient ones to the attention of their readers.

www.facebook.com/onpointbookfair

# Jejune

Definition: lacking interest or
significance or impact.

Examples: His ruminations on biology
may be jejune, but unwelcome facts
are still facts.

An example of a jejune story is a
ten minute story about someone
eating a piece of celery.

In this generation more and more
millennials may be jejune to what is
happening around the world.

# Rife

Definition: abundant.

Examples: Predictions about who will win the competition are rife, given the approach of the final episode.

It is commonly agreed that corruption and nepotism is rife within the court system.

# Acquiesce

Definition: to agree without protesting.

Examples: Though Mr. Smith wanted to stay outside and work in his garage, when his wife told him to come inside for dinner, he acquiesced to her demands.

The committee will acquiesce in any decision on which it is not fully informed.

# Repudiate

Definition: to reject, refuse
to accept.

Examples: The logical and just
thing was to repudiate the enormous
debt incurred by the monarchy.

A union has the power to repudiate
action purportedly done in its name
and on its behalf, but there are
stringent conditions.

# Alacrity

Definition: eagerness, speed.

Examples: Having studied really hard last night, the student took the exam with alacrity.

The boy jumped up and down with alacrity as he inched closer to the candy store.

# Perusal

Definition: a careful examination,
review.

Examples: They just showed up
once a quarter for a round of golf
and a casual perusal of the books.

Archives and libraries and museums
have any amount of information and
documents available for perusal.

# Fractious

Definition: troublesome or
irritable.

Examples: Although the child
insisted he wasn't tired, his
fractious behavior convinced
everyone present that it was time
to put him to bed.

People with pain can be fractious
and difficult, and elderly people
may not be paragons of charm and
cheerfulness.

# Indolent

Definition: lazy.

Examples: As a teenager he was mature in the sense that he knew his way around town, but like all 15-year-olds he could be pretty indolent.

His corpulent figure and indolent manner belied ambition and a keen political intelligence.

# Meticulous

Definition: extremely careful with details.

Examples: The ornate needlework in the bride's gown was a product of meticulous handiwork.

The painter gave a meticulous attention to detail.

I am trying to be meticulous in my sentences before sending them to my boss.

POINT
OK FAIR

NPOINTEXECUTIVECENTER.COM

ONE DAY – 100 LOCAL AUTHORS, PUBLISHERS, PODCASTERS, PUBLICATIONS, VENDORS, SPEAKERS & MORE ...CELEBRATING THE ART OF WRITING!

# Implacable

Definition: incapable or being appeased or mitigated.

Examples: The man who is supposed to be protecting them is somehow their fiercest and most implacable enemy.

But we also learn that the downside of her implacable self-belief was a certain unapproachability.

# Balter

Definition: to dance artlessly,
without particular grace or skill
but usually with enjoyment.

Example: Our owner loves to balter
around the office, much like Elaine
on the Seinfeld show.

# Modicum

Definition: a small amount of
something.

Examples: I was pleased with the
overall response and I think we
collectively felt a modicum of
relief.

Unable to garner even a modicum of
support for his plan, he conceded to
follow the others.

# Fractious

Definition: troublesome or
irritable.

Examples:  People with pain
can be fractious and difficult,
and elderly people may not be
paragons of charm and cheerfulness.

Some of them can be very demanding
and ungrateful, even obstreperous
and fractious.

WORD OF THE WEEK

•

# Nadir

Definition: the lowest point of something.

Examples: My day was boring, by the nadir came when my new car was stolen.

Because employees are terribly worried about losing their positions, company morale has reached a nadir.

# Ennui

Definition: the feeling of being bored by something tedious.

Examples: I managed to fight off ennui and squeeze out an analysis of sorts after all.

One man's ennui is another man's earner, which is why we have accountants, cleaners and cooks.

# Panacea

Definition: a remedy for all ills
or difficulties.

Examples: Doctors wish there was a
simple panacea for every disease,
but sadly there is not.

The snake oil salesman of the Old
West typically hawked a bottled
elixir of questionable content,
claiming its value as a panacea.

# Erudite

Definition: learned.

Examples: My English teacher is such an erudite scholar that he has translated some of the most difficult and abstruse Old English poetry.

The power of his book lies not in prescription, but rather in his acute, erudite and provocative historical analysis

# Repudiate

Definition: to reject, refuse to accept.

Examples: Tom made a strong case for an extension of his curfew, but his mother repudiated it with a few biting words.

Because I want to avoid the conflict between my two sisters, I repudiate their argument.

# Biblioklept

Definition: one who steals books;
a book thief.

Examples: I can never find the
book I'm looking because my sister
is a biblioklept.

Jane Eyre is missing which means
the biblioklept is on the loose.

# Jouska

Definition: a hypothetical
conversation you play out in
your head.

Example: He spent more time in
jouska than in reality that is
conversations skills were quite
boring.

# Zenith

Definition: the highest point reached in the heavens by a celestial body; a culminating point.

Examples: The zenith of our conversation was when you described your visit to Belize.

The Sun reached its zenith while we were enjoying our lunch at the park.

www.facebook.com/onpointbookfair

# Octothorpe

Definition:   the symbol #

Examples: If you want to sound
more educated, use "octothorpe"
instead of "hashtag".

When I look on Facebook, I see
an abundance of octothorpes.

# Boondoggle

Definition: work of little to no value done merely to look busy.

Examples: In my opinion, the tax-rebate idea is a huge boondoggle and is what desperate politicians come up with to make us feel like they are doing something.

A major bill may contain dozens of bridges to nowhere, or boondoggle favors to some deep-pocketed donor.

# Quixotic

Definition: foolishly impractical especially in the pursuit of ideals; often marked by rash lofty romantic ideas or extravagantly chivalrous action.

Examples: It's a bit quixotic to expect that all movies will have a happy ending.

Her quixotic notions of romance often cause problems in her real life relationships.

# Sycophant

Definition: one who flatters for self-gain.

Examples: Though, like most of his order, zealous for monarchy, he was no sycophant.

He's a sycophant social climber who's not beyond using a little groveling to ingratiate himself with someone who advance his opportunities.

# Earthshine

Definition: sunlight reflected by the Earth that illuminates the dark part of the moon.

Examples: The Hubble telescope captured amazing photos of the moon while it was embraced by the earthshine.

He lights up my life like the earthshine illuminates the dark side of the moon.

56

# Loquacious

Definition:  given to fluent or
excessive talk.

Examples: My mother in law can be
quite loquacious at times.

I'd rather appear to be shy and
well-liked than to annoy others
with loquacious behavior.

www.facebook.com/onpointbookfair

# Cloying

Definition: overly sweet.

Examples: The chicken and fruits, combined with honey and lemon, were sweet without being cloying, and struck the exact balance between tangy and savory.

The desserts were similarly cloying, except for a plate of crumbly, warm chocolate-chip cookies, served with a bowl of coconut milk.

# Wrest pin

Definition: a pin in a stringed
musical instrument around which
the ends of the strings are coiled
and by which the instrument is
tuned.

Examples: The E string on my guitar
will remain out of tune until I can
replace the wrest pin.

His daughter's love was the wrest
pin to which his heartstrings were
attached.

# Aplomb

Definition: complete and confident composure or self-assurance.

Examples: Nicole Kidman performed with aplomb in her recent role as the president's wife.

I hope that with all the care given in preparing her speech that she will deliver it tomorrow with aplomb.

# Liminal

Definition: barely perceptible
or capable of eliciting a
response; of, relating to, or
being an intermediate state,
phase, or condition.

Examples: There was dirt on the
bottom of her skirt, but since it
was liminal, I didn't mention it.

His face came to mind in that
liminal moment between waking
and sleeping.

# Staid

Definition: sedate, serious, self-restrained.

Examples: I envisioned a staid, quiet event in which people would come and go in silence.

This site will no doubt be jarring to the casual observer more familiar with staid academic websites.

# Agelast

Definition:   a person who never laughs.

Examples: It's no fun being around George; he's such an agelast.

No one will ever call my husband an agelast because he finds humor in everything.

# Panacea

Definition: a remedy for all ills
or difficulties.

Examples: Some researchers contend
that sympathetic nerve blocks are
not the panacea they are made out
to be.

The drugs are not a panacea, but
they do improve quality of life and
boost life expectancy.

# Metanoia

Definition: a transformative
change of heart; especially,
a spiritual conversion.

Examples: She was speechless at
his drastic course change and
wondered what could have caused
such a metanoia.

The surprising metanoia of
Ebenezer Scrooge is often
pondered at Christmas.

# Numinous

Definition: supernatural or mysterious; filled with a sense of the presence of divinity; appealing to the higher emotions or to the aesthetic sense.

Examples: The entire church was silent as the numinous atmosphere in the sanctuary held everyone captive.

As she sang the words of the beautiful song, the numinous melody brought the audience to tears.

# Obsequious

Definition: excessively compliant or submissive.

Examples: It wasn't so much obsequious as deferent, something that was most unusual in a politician.

Thus approached, I would smile benignly and direct the appropriately obsequious customer toward the objects of his desiring.

# Lexophile

Definition: those that have a
love for words.

Examples:  you can tune a piano,
but you can't tuna fish.

To write with a broken pencil is
pointless.

England has no kidney bank, but it
does have a Liverpool.
.
A thief who stole a calendar got
twelve months.

When the smog lifts in Los Angeles
U.C.L.A.

I got some batteries that were given
out free of charge.

A dentist and a manicurist married.
They fought tooth and nail.

A will is a dead giveaway.

With her marriage, she got a new
name and a dress.

Police were summoned to a daycare
center where a three-year-old was
resisting a rest.

Did you hear about the fellow
whose entire left side was cut
off? He's all right now.

A bicycle can't stand alone; it's
just two tired.

The guy who fell onto an upholstery
machine last week is now fully
recovered.
He had a photographic memory, but
it was never fully developed.

When she saw her first strands of
gray hair, she thought she'd dye.

Acupuncture is a jab well done.
That's the point of it.

I didn't like my beard at first.
Then it grew on me.

Did you hear about the crossed eyed
teacher who lost her job because
she couldn't control her pupils?

When you get a bladder infection, urine trouble.
I stayed up all night to see where the sun went, and then it dawned on me.

I'm reading a book about anti-gravity. I just can't put it down.

Those who get too big for their pants will be totally exposed in the end.

Do you have a favorite lexophile? Send it to us at info@onpointexecutivecenter.com to be featured on our FB page!

www.facebook.com/onpointbookfair

WORD OF THE WEEK

www.facebookcom/onpointbookfair

On Point Book Fair is hosted by
On Point Executive Center

3030 N. Rocky Point Drive W., #150
Tampa, FL 33607
www.onpointexecutivecenter.com